Voices of Freedom

The Gettysburg Address

Karen Price Hossell

Heinemann
LIBRARY

Chicago, Illinois

© 2006 Heinemann Library
a division of Reed Elsevier, Inc.
Chicago, Illinois
Customer Service: 888-454-2279
Visit our website at www.heinemannlibrary.com

Printed in China by WKT Company Limited
10 09 08 07 06
10 9 8 7 6 5 4 3 2 1

Library of Congress Cataloging-in-Publication Data:
Price Hossell, Karen, 1957-
    The Gettysburg address / Karen Price Hossell.
       p. cm. -- (Voices of freedom)
    Includes bibliographical references (p.   ) and index.
    ISBN 1-4034-6812-5 (hc) -- ISBN 1-4034-6817-6 (pb)
    1. Lincoln, Abraham, 1809-1865. Gettysburg address--Juvenile
literature. 2. Lincoln, Abraham, 1809-1865--Juvenile literature.
I. Title. II. Series: Price Hossell, Karen, 1957-   . Voices of
freedom.
E475.55.P75 2005
973.7'349--dc22
                                2005006264

Acknowledgments
The publisher would like to thank the following for permission to reproduce photographs:
AP Wide World Photo p. 36 (Seth Perlman); Corbis pp. 6 (Nathan Benn), 7 (Kelly-Mooney Photography), 8 (Medford
Historical Society Collection), 9, 11, 12, 15, 17 (Bettmann), 20 (Bettmann), 21, 23, 24, 26, 27, 28 (Bettmann), 29,
30, 31 (Lester Lefkowitz), 32 (Medford Historical Society Collection), 37 (Bettmann), 38 (Bettmann), 39, 40, 41;
Heinemann Library p. 43 (Jill Birschbach); Library of Congress pp. title, 4, 5, 13, 14, 16, 18, 19, 25, 33, 34, 35, 45;
North Wind Picture Archives p. 44 (Nancy Carter); The Granger Collection p. 10.

Cover image of Lincoln reproduced with permission of Corbis.

Every effort has been made to contact copyright holders of any material reproduced in this book. Any omissions will
be rectified in subsequent printings if notice is given to the publisher

Some words are shown in bold, **like this**. You can find out what they
mean by looking in the glossary.

Contents

Recording Important Events

One way to know about what happened in the past is by reading documents written by people who were witnesses to history. Some of these documents are letters about events written by people who were there when the events occurred. Other kinds of important historical documents are **memoirs** written by people who were in a war or by leaders after they left office. Records of history that provide a firsthand account of an event are called primary sources. When several primary sources of the same event are gathered together, they can provide us with a more complete story of the event.

Executive Mansion,

Washington, _____ , 186 .

Four score and seven years ago our fathers brought forth, upon this continent, a new nation, conceived in liberty, and dedicated to the proposition that "all men are created equal"

Now we are engaged in a great civil war, testing whether that nation, or any nation so conceived, and so dedicated, can long endure. We are met on a great battle field of that war. We have come to dedicate a portion of it, as a final rest-ing place for those who died here, that the nation might live. This we may, in all propriety do. But, in a larger sense, we can not dedicate—we can not consecrate—we can not hallow, this ground— The brave men, living and dead, who struggled here, have hallowed it, far above our poor power to add or detract. The world will little note, nor long remember what we say here; while it can never forget what they did here.

It is rather for us, the living, to stand here,

This is the Nicolay version of the Gettysburg Address.

Primary sources also include **drafts** of speeches and official papers that were carefully planned. The people involved in the planning and writing of these documents were often careful to make sure the words in the documents expressed their exact thoughts. Other kinds of primary sources include videos or sound recordings. They can be of events such as the first man on the moon or the events of the attack on the World Trade Center on September 11, 2001.

Primary sources are important because they tell us in the words of people who lived through a time or event what happened. Most written documents contain some of a writer's opinion. As time passes, opinions of an event often change. For example, a person writing about the Civil War today would probably have a different opinion of the events than a person who was writing as the fighting was going on.

Knowing what people thought about an event at the time can help us to better understand the event.

This letter to Albert Hodges, an editor in Kentucky, outlines Lincoln's views on slavery. It is an example of a primary source.

Secondary sources

Another category of sources are those written by people who have studied primary sources. These are secondary sources. Scholars study these and write their own books and articles based on their research. When you write a research paper for school you are creating a secondary source. However, if in the future someone wants to study how students wrote research papers in the 21st Century, your paper could become a primary source.

Storing and Preserving Historical Documents

Protecting the primary and secondary sources that make up our historical records is so important that those records are kept in buildings devoted to that purpose. The records are kept in buildings where people can enjoy them and study them. In the United States two of the best-known archives are the National Archives and Records Administration, or NARA, and the Library of Congress. An archive is a place where documents are stored.

The Library of Congress

The Library of Congress is in Washington, D.C. It is a federal institution and also the largest library in the world. Its collection is available to members of Congress as well as to the rest of the American public. The Library of Congress holds about 120 million items, including maps, books, and photographs.

The National Archives and Records Administration (NARA)

The original documents in the NARA collection provide a history of the United States government. It houses paper documents and films, photographs, posters, sound and video recordings, and other types of government records. They also tell the story of American settlement, industry, and farming. In fact, documents and other **artifacts** detailing almost every aspect of American history can be found in the NARA collection.

The technique being used to restore this book is from the sixteenth century.

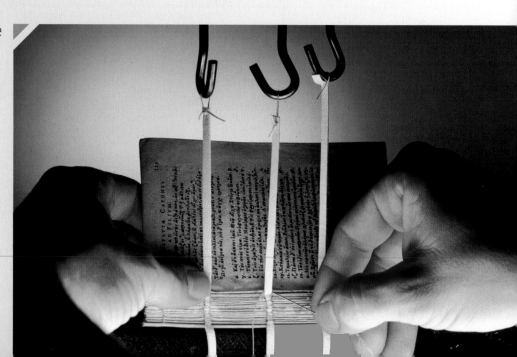

Among the documents stored in the NARA is a group of documents called the Charters of Freedom. They include the United States Constitution, the Bill of Rights, and the Declaration of Independence. These historical records are on display in the public area of the NARA.

In 1998 **conservators** at the NARA became concerned about the condition of the Charters of Freedom, so they closed the public exhibit. Then they carefully removed each document from its bulletproof and fireproof glass case and closely examined it for damage. They found that in some cases the ink had faded from the parchment, so they had to repair the document using special techniques.

Special storage facilities

Other paper records in the NARA are stored in specially designed boxes. Because paper gets darker over time, documents can become hard to read. The documents are kept in special boxes that keep the paper from darkening. The boxes are stored in fireproof, locked stacks. The temperature and humidity, or wetness, in NARA storage areas are carefully controlled, because heat and humidity can damage documents.

Conservators know how to protect tape recordings, videotapes, photographs, and other kinds of artifacts. In the future, people will be able to look at these documents just as we look at the Declaration of Independence and other historical records.

This photograph shows the interior of the main reading room of the Library of Congress.

What Is the Gettysburg Address?

On a cool November day in 1863, a crowd of at least 15,000 people stood in a field just outside Gettysburg, Pennsylvania, and listened to speaker Edward Everett deliver a two-hour speech. The reason for the speech was the **dedication** of a cemetery for those who had died in a battle nearby.

People were restless as Everett continued to speak. But when he finished they looked forward to hearing the next speaker. They had come to honor their sons and husbands and brothers who had been killed in the Battle of Gettysburg, but they had also come to hear the next man on the program. He was President Abraham Lincoln, the leader of the United States.

This photograph from 1863 shows the countryside that surrounds Gettysburg.

One of the few known photographs of the day Lincoln gave his address at Gettysburg.

Lincoln walked to the **podium**. He was a tall, thin man. Most in the audience were too far away to see his beard or his sparkling gray eyes. There were no microphones or sound systems in those days, so the crowd gathered closer to hear his voice. During his short speech, President Lincoln was interrupted by applause five times.

The speech Lincoln gave that day lasted only three minutes and was only 372 words long. But that speech is one of the most famous and most important in American history. It brought together a nation that was broken and hurting, divided into two parts—North and South. Lincoln's speech gave Americans hope that one day the United States would be as strong and united as its founders had dreamed it would be.

The Beginning of Slavery

In some ways, the United States had always been divided by North and South. The North had large cities such as Philadelphia, New York, and Boston. While many people made their money on large- and medium-size farms in the North, even more people worked as **merchants** and craftspeople.

This illustration is of an 18th Century tobacco plantation in Virginia.

The South was somewhat different. It had large cities, such as Richmond, Charleston, and New Orleans. But the South also had acres and acres of vast **plantations**. In the years when the American colonies had belonged to England, the land that made up the plantations was given to royal relatives or people who had done favors for the king or queen. The owners passed the plantations on to their sons, who often came to live in America, or sold parts or all of their land to wealthy Americans. But no matter who owned them, plantation owners, or planters as they were called, always hoped that plantations would make money.

Early on colonists in the south discovered a crop they could sell in England and parts of Europe—tobacco. They harvested and dried the tobacco, then packed it into barrels called hogsheads and shipped it across the Atlantic Ocean to England. Planters made a great deal of money from tobacco, but to grow as much tobacco and make as much money as they could, they needed cheap labor—workers who would not demand a lot of money. The cheapest labor they could find was slaves.

The slave trade grew until it was a thriving business. Not long after the colonies declared their independence from Great Britain and became the United States, almost 700,000 slaves worked in the nation.

Slave traders sailed ships to Africa, kidnapped people there, chained them together, and forced them onto cramped, filthy ships. They sailed the Africans across the Atlantic and sold them in the United States as slaves. Plantation owners and their managers went to slave markets in cities such as Charleston, South Carolina, and New Orleans, Louisiana, to buy slaves to work on their land.

Reactions to slavery in the United States were mixed. Many people thought it was wrong but did nothing to stop it. They knew that the **economy** of the country depended on the **exports** slaves helped to produce. Many people thought that slavery was not completely wrong because, they believed, black people were not as intelligent as whites and did not deserve to have the same kinds of lives as whites. They believed that blacks could not learn and should be treated like children.

Still others firmly believed that slavery was wrong. They worked to end slavery and helped slaves who tried to escape. These people were called **abolitionists**. While there were abolitionists from the early days of slavery, most did not speak out until the 1800s.

This depiction of the slave trade is from 1830. The U.S. Capitol can be seen in the upper right corner.

Federal Rights vs. States' Rights

The plantation system thrived in the South in the 1700s and early 1800s. Tobacco continued to be an important crop, but it used up the soil quickly and planters had to clear new fields for crops every few years. With the invention of the cotton gin in 1793, cotton became an important crop, and hundreds of plantations throughout the South grew cotton. Slaves spent up to fifteen hours a day in the hot sun pulling cotton from the prickly plants and stuffing it into sacks. Another crop that grew well in the American South was rice, particularly in South Carolina. Rice planters owned many slaves, too.

All of these crops made money for the Southern United States, and the nation depended on these **exports**. In 1808, early in the life of the nation, **Congress** passed a law that ended the slave trade, but not slavery. Planters could still buy, sell, and own slaves, but taking slaves from Africa and selling them in the United States was no longer legal.

This painting shows a working cotton plantation.

A great experiment

The United States government and the Constitution upon which it is based were considered by even the founding fathers to be an experiment. Everyone in the United States was part of that experiment, especially those who could vote and the people they elected. So from its first days, people questioned how this experiment would work. One of the biggest questions concerned the amount of power the **federal** government should have and how much power state governments should have. Today we view the United States as one, united country. At the time though, individual states were seen as being more independent. Many states were concerned that Congress, which is part of the federal government, made too many laws for them. Those who wanted stronger "state rights" thought Congress had too much power over each state.

An example of this was when Congress outlawed slavery in new United States **territories**. Southerners believed the federal government had no right to outlaw slavery in a territory. They saw this as **unconstitutional** and felt that the federal government was slowly taking over the rights of states to make their own laws. By the time Abraham Lincoln ran for President in 1860, several southern states were thinking about leaving the United States and becoming independent. This act is called **secession**.

Eli Whitney's cotton gin changed the course of history by making cotton a profitable crop.

Abraham Lincoln

Abraham Lincoln was born in Kentucky in 1809. He lived so far out in the country that he could not get to school easily. But he liked to read and taught himself enough about law to become a lawyer.

In the 1830s Lincoln was elected to the state **legislature** in Illinois. The second time he ran for the legislature, he traveled with other candidates on horseback from one town to another, making speeches to small gatherings and large crowds to convince them to vote for him—and they did.

The legislature met only for a few months a year. Lincoln practiced law the rest of the year. He opened a law office in 1837 in Springfield, Illinois. As he practiced law and argued cases in court, he polished his public speaking skills.

He also learned to **debate** while in Springfield. With other businessmen, Lincoln spent evenings gathered around a woodstove in the back of his friend Joshua Speed's general store. The men argued and debated about political issues such as states' rights and slavery.

Lincoln continued his political career in Illinois and in 1846 was elected to the United States House of Representatives. He and his young family moved to Washington, D.C. While in the House of Representatives, Lincoln made several speeches. He also argued a case as a lawyer before the Illinois Supreme Court.

Abraham Lincoln, shortly before he was nominated to serve in the Illinois State Senate.

Here is Abraham Lincoln, nine years after the photo at left.

Lincoln left politics in 1849, but in 1856 he helped to form the new Republican Party. The Republicans were an antislavery party, and by this time, Lincoln was beginning to speak out against slavery. In 1858, he was nominated to be a Republican senator from Illinois. He ran against Democrat Stephen A. Douglas. The two men agreed to debate each other seven times in cities throughout Illinois. In debates, one person speaks and then allows the other person to speak on their side of the issue.

Know It!

Lincoln's young son Willie died on February 20, 1862, in the White House. Most historians believe he died of a fever brought on by polluted White House water.

The Lincoln-Douglas Debates

Stephen A. Douglas was a popular Democrat who ran against Abraham Lincoln for senator. Many people already knew Douglas, but most did not know who Lincoln was. They could read about him in the newspaper, but since this was long before television and the Internet, the only other way they could hear his views, and the only way they could see him, was to be in the audience to hear him speak.

When Lincoln and Douglas started their series of **debates** in Ottawa, Illinois on August 21, 1858, a crowd gathered to listen. The crowd knew that Lincoln and Douglas were going to speak on the main issues of the day. These issues included slavery and whether it should be allowed in the new states and **territories** in the West.

Lincoln was against slavery. He did not say it should be outlawed in the states in which it was established, he did think it should be outlawed in new states and territories. Douglas thought that slavery should continue, and that territories should decide for themselves whether to allow it. He also believed that it was proper for whites to rule blacks.

Even at the first debate in Ottawa, Lincoln was greeted by loud cheers, and he had to wait until people stopped cheering before he spoke. Lincoln included lots of humor in his speech, and people laughed at his jokes throughout it. The speeches both men gave were long, but the audience listened closely, because the subjects they spoke about were so important to Americans at the time.

Few people remember that Stephen Douglas actually won the Lincoln-Douglas debates.

By the end of the debates, most people in the country knew who Lincoln was. He did not win the election. Douglas became the next senator from Illinois, but Lincoln's success at speaking brought him a great deal of attention.

This illustration shows the Lincoln-Douglas debates. Notice the crowd listening carefully to Lincoln's speech.

Know It!

During the time period of the Lincoln-Douglas debates, three new states were admitted into the Union. Minnesota became a state in 1858, Oregon in 1859, and Kansas in 1861.

An Eyewitness Account of Lincoln at the Debates

Lincoln's law partner, William H. Herndon, wrote about Lincoln's speaking skills during this first debate. He said that Lincoln did not pace back and forth on the stage, but instead stood still. At six-foot-four, Lincoln was much taller than Stephen Douglas. Lincoln sometimes held onto his lapel when he spoke, or clasped his hands behind his back. He sometimes raised his hands to the skies when he wanted to emphasize the importance of what he was saying. At first Lincoln's voice, said Herndon, was "shrill and piping," but as he continued to speak, he relaxed, and his voice became lower and "musical."

Lincoln's Nomination

After Lincoln lost the election to Douglas, he decided to go back and work hard at his law firm. But he had become so interested in politics that he knew he wanted to keep working for the Republican Party. A presidential election was going to take place in 1860, and Lincoln wanted to make sure a Republican won.

The Republicans had several people to choose from for their presidential candidate. Stephen A. Douglas was the Democratic candidate, and the Republicans needed a strong man to run against Douglas. Lincoln began to travel the country speaking against Douglas's ideas on slavery and other issues. Some people thought Lincoln should run against Douglas, but Lincoln did not think he would make a good president. He reminded people that he had only one year of formal schooling, and that he had only been a state **legislator**. Many other possible candidates, he pointed out, had been to good colleges and had been senators or governors.

Lincoln's first name is mispelled on this campaign banner.

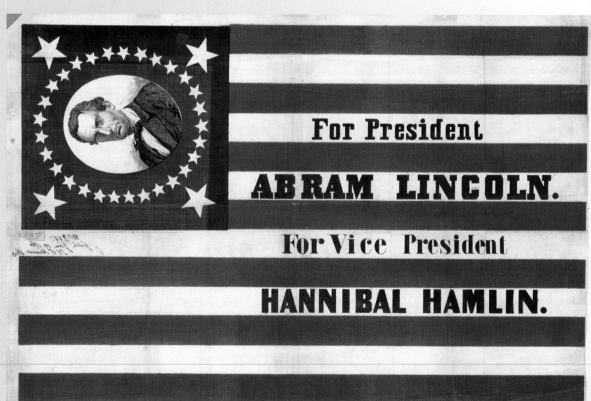

For President
ABRAM LINCOLN.

For Vice President
HANNIBAL HAMLIN.

This is part of a draft of Lincoln's first inaugural address.

Several newspapers published articles that said Lincoln should run for president. One of the reasons so many people thought he would be good was because of his speeches. In New York City, for example, he spoke to a group of Republicans. At first, they saw the tall, rough man up on stage and were not impressed. Lincoln bought a new suit for the occasion, but the suit was made by a country tailor in Illinois, not a stylish one in New York. The audience saw his messy hair and large hands and feet and wondered why they had heard so many wonderful things about such an awkward-looking man.

But then Lincoln began to speak, and soon everyone in the audience realized why he was so popular. He meant what he said when he was speaking, and he made the audience laugh with his humor. They could tell his ideas were well researched and thought out. By the end of the speech in New York, the crowd was cheering loudly for Lincoln. The speech he gave that day in February of 1860 was published the next day in four newspapers, and was published in a pamphlet.

The Republican Convention took place in May of 1860 in Chicago. Lincoln did not go, but he was nominated as the Republican candidate for president. The next day, a group of men from the Republican Party came to Lincoln's house to discuss the idea with him. Four days later, Lincoln agreed to run for president.

The Nation Divides

Lincoln was elected president in November of 1860. Most of his votes came from states in the North. People in southern states did not vote for Lincoln because of his views on slavery. Many feared that with Lincoln as president, slavery would be outlawed, and as a result, their **plantations** would lose workers and money.

For years leading up to Lincoln's election, the southern states had often threatened that if the United States **Congress** passed laws it did not like, they would **secede**. This means that they would declare themselves out of the United States. They would become free and independent nations that governed themselves.

With Lincoln's win, some states felt they had no choice but to secede. Lincoln's hatred of slavery and his speeches insisting that it not be allowed in new states and **territories** proved to them that once he was president, he would make slavery illegal. If that happened, their entire way of life would change.

Secession

On December 20, 1860, only about six weeks after Lincoln was elected president, the state of South Carolina seceded from the United States. Lincoln was not yet president officially and would not be until his **inauguration** in January 1861. The man who was president, James Buchanan, did nothing when South Carolina seceded.

When the Confederate states seceded they printed up their own money.

More southern states followed South Carolina's lead. Before Lincoln's inauguration, six more states seceded-Alabama, Florida, Georgia, Louisiana, Mississippi, and Texas. Buchanan still did nothing. The new states formed a group they called the Confederacy. Their new president, they declared, was Jefferson Davis.

The northern states remained in the United States, and because they considered themselves so united, they called themselves the Union. They would be led by the **federal** government of the United States, with Abraham Lincoln as their president. The Union Army was also called the Federal Army.

The division of the United States put Lincoln in a terrible situation. It would be a great test of the strength of the United States Constitution and of the government it supported. In the next four years, the country would be torn apart by the worst violence and fighting in its history.

Jefferson Davis was elected President of the Confederacy.

Jefferson Davis

Jefferson Davis was born in Kentucky in 1809 and grew up to be a soldier, politician, and Mississippi planter. He was a United States Senator until Mississippi seceded from the Union. In 1861, the Confederacy elected him president, although once he became their leader he did not get along with many Confederate generals. Davis was captured by Union forces at the end of the war in 1865 and spent two years in prison, then was released. He spent most of the years before his death in 1889 writing about the Confederacy.

The Civil War

The division of the North and South into the Union and Confederacy tore the United States apart. While the Union firmly believed that its government was in charge of all the states, including those in the Confederacy, the Confederacy refused to obey the Union government. It formed its own government, with its own army.

The Confederacy grows

In the spring of 1861, four more states **seceded** from the Union—Virginia, North Carolina, Arkansas, and Tennessee. Now the Confederacy had eleven states, the Union twenty-three. The Confederacy set up its capital in Richmond, Virginia.

After these states seceded, the Union began to worry that the states that bordered the Confederacy would secede, as well. The Confederates worked to persuade these states—Delaware, Missouri, Kentucky, and Maryland—to join them. But the border states remained in the Union throughout the war.

This map shows the states that seceded from the Union.

Fort Sumter

The Union had two forts in the South. One was Fort Pickens in Florida's Pensacola Bay. The other was Fort Sumter in Charleston Harbor, just outside Charleston, South Carolina. The Confederate Army did not like that a Union-controlled fort was sitting right outside Charleston. On April 10, 1861, the Confederates decided to order the Union troops in Fort Sumter to leave, and threatened to bomb the fort if they stayed. The troops remained, and the Confederate Army's boats surrounded the fort and **bombarded** it. Finally, Major Anderson, the head officer at the fort, surrendered to Confederate troops on April 13.

With this battle, the Civil War had begun. It was to become the only war fought on American soil since the birth of the nation and the only war where Americans fought Americans. More than 600,000 Americans died in the war. More American soldiers died in the Civil War than in all other wars in United States history combined.

Soldiers from Conneticut at the seige of Yorktown, Virginia.

Matthew Brady (1823–1896)

Many of the photos we have of Lincoln, the Civil War, and the Union leaders were taken by a man named Matthew Brady. Brady was an early pioneer in photography and a staunch supporter of the Republican party and the Union. Lincoln is said to have told friends that "Brady and the Copper Union speech made me president." Brady spent over $100,000 of his own money on creating prints of the Civil War. He expected the government to reimburse him after the war. The government refused to do so and Brady died bankrupt.

The Commander-in-Chief

The United States Constitution states that the president also serves as commander-in-chief of the **military**. During times of peace, this usually means that the president makes big decisions regarding the military, but leaves the everyday issues and problems to the military officers under him. During times of war, presidents can become very involved in day-to-day military operations, or they can continue to rely on the decisions of key military leaders.

Lincoln's role as commander-in-chief was difficult. The war was being fought not in some faraway land or on the ocean. It was being fought on American soil—and sometimes only a few hundred miles from the White House. In the 1700s, Americans had worked hard and fought and died to keep the United States free from foreign rule. Now that nation was divided. Americans disagreed over how they should be governed and what kinds of laws they should live by, and they were killing each other by the thousands.

Lincoln was very involved in conducting the war. He wanted to be able to rely on military leaders who were under him, such as General George B. McClellan, who led the Union Army of the Potomac. But McClellan often hesitated to take action. This frustrated Lincoln, as well as **Congress**, and Lincoln felt he had to become even more involved as a result. Most of his generals did not like that he did this. The generals knew they had more military experience than Lincoln. The leader of the Confederacy, Jefferson Davis, was an experienced soldier who knew how to lead an army.

President Lincoln is shown with soldiers at Antietam in 1862.

This telegraph office is from shortly after the Civil War. The telgraph allowed armies to communicate in a new way.

Lincoln tried to overcome the gap in his experience by reading books about military **strategy**. Still, many questioned whether he was capable of commanding the military. Sometimes, government leaders complained Lincoln only offered suggestions instead of giving commands.

On the wall in Lincoln's office in the White House were maps of locations where battles were taking place. He liked to stand in front of the maps and study them, following the stages of battles.

The Telegraph

One way Lincoln kept in touch with what was happening on the battlefield was through the telegraph. The telegraph was first used in 1844, and by 1850 12,000 miles of telegraph wires were strung on poles all throughout the United States. Messages could be sent over the wires through a device using a special code that was picked up by telegraph stations along the way. Both armies, Union and Confederate, actually traveled with telegraph equipment. They would stop near telegraph poles, then hook up their wire to a telegraph pole and send messages through the wires.

The War Department was near the White House, and during the Civil War Lincoln would visit the telegraph room in the War Department every day he could. There, Lincoln would read messages from generals about the progress of the war, and he would send messages to them on the battlefield.

The War Continues

Union leaders were upset as, battle after battle, their army kept losing. At one point, Lincoln thought maybe he could do a better job, and he thought about taking over the army himself.

But after Lincoln replaced some of his staff and became more used to commanding the army, things began to improve for the Union. Lincoln and his advisers managed to organize the armies and make their commands clear to their generals.

This illustration of the siege of Vicksburg was created shortly after the battle.

In the days leading up to the Battle of Gettysburg, several violent battles left thousands dead on both sides. One took place on the banks of the Rappahannock River in Fredericksburg, Virginia. Another occurred in Tennessee between the Union Army of the Tennessee, led by General Ulysses S. Grant, and the Confederates. That battle resulted in the deaths of 13,000 Union soldiers and almost 12,000 Confederates.

Vicksburg

Grant then moved on to Vicksburg, Mississippi, which was high on a bluff on the Mississippi River. The city was an important one because while the Confederates held the city, they could stop any ship going up or down river, therefore controlling the flow of supplies. In January 1863 General Grant led 45,000 soldiers to just above Vicksburg. The army took almost three months to come up with a plan to take the city. Finally, in March, he came up with an idea. He marched his army around the city, taking the small towns and villages that surrounded it. The Confederate troops there were trapped. They fought back, and the **siege** continued until the Confederates surrendered on July 4, 1863. It took months, but the Union Army had won a great victory at Vicksburg. At exactly the same time, another battle was being fought in the small Pennsylvania town of Gettysburg.

Ulysses S. Grant

Ulysses Grant (1822–1855) was born in Ohio. He went to West Point Military Academy. At the start of the Civil War he was working in his father's leather store. The Governor of Ohio appointed him to lead a volunteer regiment of the army. He did this so well that he continued to be appointed to higher posts. In 1864 Lincoln appointed Grant General in Chief of the Army. In 1865 the Confederate general, Robert E. Lee surrendered to him. Grant served as President of the United States from 1869 to 1877.

Ulysses Grant rose quickly through the ranks of the Union Army.

The Battle of Gettysburg

In early June of 1863, Robert E. Lee led 75,000 Confederate troops into Union territory when the Confederate Army of Northern Virginia crossed the Potomac River into Maryland. In May, another Confederate division was victorious in Chancellorsville, Virginia, and felt confident they could push north. Reacting to Lee's move, Union Major General George Meade marched the Army of the Potomac division of the Union Army south to stop them.

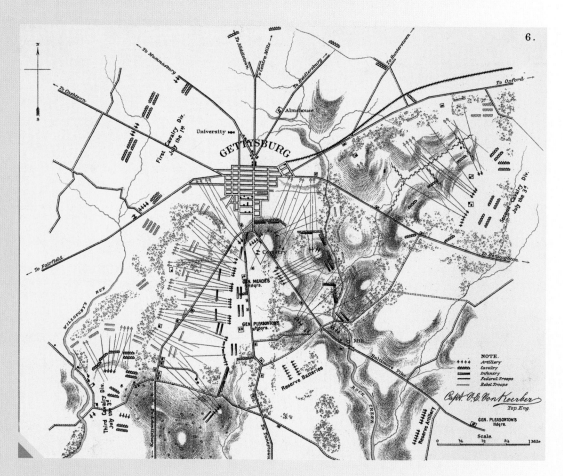

This battle map of Gettysburg shows where the cavalry and infantry units were positioned.

On July 1, Lee sent a few men ahead to Gettysburg to demand supplies from shopkeepers. Lee told them not to make trouble, but on the return trip to the Confederate camp, the soldiers met up with some Union soldiers and fought. One Union soldier was killed. Confederate forces separated into smaller units and moved into other parts of Pennsylvania—some even approached Harrisburg, the state capital.

The real battle began in the fields around Gettysburg. The fighting was fierce; it stopped and restarted several times. The battle lasted for three days. As it went on, wounded Union soldiers walked or were carried into town. People who lived there were horrified at the violence taking place on their doorstep, but most pitched in to help the wounded.

On the second day of fighting, more than 6,000 men from both armies were killed. As evening approached, thousands more injured soldiers lay on the battlefield. On day three, after six hours of nonstop fighting, the Confederate Army retreated—but they did not flee. General Lee decided to attack where he thought the Union Army was the weakest.

At one o'clock on July 3, Lee ordered 150 guns to fire at once. For almost an hour, both sides fired shots. When the Union Army's guns seemed to die down, about 12,000 Confederates charged them. The Union Army then fired into the line of oncoming soldiers. The Confederates finally backed off and began moving south. But thousands of dead, dying, and wounded men remained behind.

Robert E. Lee

Like his Union counterpart, General Grant, Robert E. Lee (1807–1870) attended West Point Military Academy. He graduated second in his class. Although he did not believe in slavery, Lee resigned from the United States Army rather than fight against his native Virginia. He became Brigadier General of the Confederate Army. Both the Union and the Confederacy admired his skill as a general. After the war he became president of Washington College.

Robert E. Lee did not believe in slavery, but fought for the Confederacy to support his native Virginia.

The Cemetery

During the fighting at Gettysburg, both armies tried to bury most of their dead. But after the battle, they left Gettysburg to plan their next move.

The armies left behind about 21,000 wounded soldiers in makeshift hospitals in schools, churches, and even homes. People from all around Gettysburg who had heard about the battle came into town to help care for the soldiers. Every day, hundreds of these wounded soldiers died. They were buried in temporary graves where they would remain until the cemetery that Pennsylvania's governor had promised to provide was set aside and prepared. The governor had visited the battlefield in early July and instructed a lawyer from Gettysburg, David Wills, to set aside land on a hillside for the cemetery.

Six weeks later the state of Pennsylvania purchased seventeen acres of land on the hillside. Some of the money came from the **legislatures** of the eighteen states that were home to the Union soldiers who had fought. Wills asked William Saunders, a well-known landscaper, to design the layout of the cemetery and to determine how many grave sites would be needed for each state.

The bodies of about 3,500 Union soldiers who had been buried in temporary graves were moved to the new cemetery. But officials were not able to identify 1,664 of the bodies. Most of the time they knew which state the dead soldiers had come from, or the name of the soldier, but not both. Over 900 soldiers were completely unidentified—officials knew neither their name nor what state they were from.

Citizens of Gettysburg set up makeshift hospitals to help wounded soldiers.

A year after the cemetery was first planned, state legislatures had given enough money to those developing the cemetery that they were able to build a stone wall and a large iron gate around it. They also provided headstones for each grave.

When all of the Union soldiers who had died in the Battle of Gettysburg were buried in the new cemetery and most of the landscaping was completed, David Wills began to plan the consecration ceremony. The purpose of the ceremony would be to officially **dedicate** the cemetery to the memory of those who had died serving their country.

Know It!

More soldiers have been buried in Gettysburg National Cemetery since the Civil War. Today, there are more than 3,700 Civil War soldiers buried there, and all together about 7,000 soldiers are buried in the cemetery.

This picture shows Gettysburg today.

Confederate graves

Because Gettysburg was in the Union state of Pennsylvania, Confederate soldiers were buried in temporary graves there—Pennsylvanians expected Confederate states to retrieve their dead and rebury them in the South. About seven months after the battle, the Ladies Memorial Associations of the southern cities of Richmond, Savannah, and Charleston raised money and had the bodies of more than 3,000 Confederate soldiers moved. Most of them were reburied in the Hollywood Cemetery in Richmond. The rest were buried in cemeteries in or near their hometowns.

The Consecration Ceremony

The consecration ceremony was for the living as much as it was for the dead. Family members of all of the soldiers were invited to come to Gettysburg and take part. Being there, many believed, would help to heal the wound of losing a loved one and would demonstrate to the survivors that the deaths of their sons and husbands and fathers were honored.

Wills wanted to hold the ceremony on October 23, 1864. A few weeks before that date, he invited Edward Everett, the most well-known speaker of the day, to deliver a speech. Everett agreed to speak at the ceremony, but he asked that the date be changed to give him more time to prepare his speech. Wills changed the date to November 19.

A parade of soldiers at the dedication of the Soldier's National Cemetery at Gettysburg.

A few weeks later, Wills sent an invitation to President Lincoln. Wills even invited the president to stay at his house. Many historians believe that Wills did not expect Lincoln to come. After all, the president was very busy running the nation and commanding the war. But Lincoln agreed to attend the ceremony and to give a speech.

The city of Gettysburg bustled in the weeks before the ceremony. Thousands of visitors were coming to their small town, including the President of the United States.

On November 18, Lincoln arrived in town on a special train from Washington, D.C. The next morning, people gathered along Baltimore Street, which led to the cemetery, and began a solemn march to the burial ground. Lincoln, along with many other government leaders, rode on horseback.

The ceremony began at noon. In the crowd were 15,000 people who were family members or friends of the dead soldiers, or who just wanted to come to honor the dead and hear the famous men speak.

Everett's speech lasted more than two hours. He reached far back into history as he spoke, describing the funeral customs of ancient Greece. After Everett came Lincoln. In contrast to Everett, his speech lasted only two minutes. Those few words, however, made many in the crowd feel proud to be Americans and gave them hope that what their loved ones had fought and died for was special and important. Even today, Lincoln's address at Gettysburg is considered to be one of the most important speeches in American history.

Not many people remember Edward Everett today.

Edward Everett

Everett was a politician from Massachusetts who was also a church pastor. He was a member of the Massachusetts House of Representatives and then became governor of the state. Everett was also a professor of Greek literature at Harvard University and served as the president of the University from 1846 to 1849. He was United States Secretary of State from 1852 to 1853 and a United States Senator the following year. Everett died in 1865.

The Gettysburg Address

Four score and seven years ago our fathers brought forth on this continent a new nation, conceived [created] in liberty and dedicated to the proposition [idea] that all men are created equal.

A score is twenty years, so Lincoln here is talking about something that took place eighty-seven years earlier—the **Declaration of Independence** and the founding of the United States of America. In the Declaration, the nation's founders said that all people are created equal.

Now we are engaged in a great civil war, testing whether that nation or any nation so conceived and so dedicated can long endure. We are met on a great battlefield of that war. We have come to dedicate a portion of that field as a final resting-place for those who here gave their lives that that nation might live. It is altogether fitting and proper that we should do this.

Lincoln refers to the Civil War, which he says is testing the nation. The test was whether a nation can last that is built on the kind of ideas the United States was founded upon. He also talks about the great battle that occurred at Gettysburg and the fact that the people there are gathered to **dedicate** a cemetery for those who died in that battle.

Notice the crying woman at the bottom left corner of this drawing of Lincoln delivering his address.

Executive Mansion,

Washington, _____ , 186 .

Four score and seven years ago our fathers brought forth, upon this continent, a new nation, conceived in liberty, and dedicated to the proposition that "all men are created equal"

One of the copies of the Gettysburg Address.

But in a larger sense, we cannot dedicate, we cannot consecrate, we cannot hallow [make holy] this ground. The brave men, living and dead who struggled here have consecrated it far above our poor power to add or detract.

Here, Lincoln says that while it is right that they honor their dead with this ceremony, they really cannot make the ground holy. Lincoln is saying that those who died there have already made it holier than anyone else can.

The world will little note nor long remember what we say here, but it can never forget what they did here. It is for us the living rather to be dedicated here to the unfinished work which they who fought here have thus far so nobly advanced. It is rather for us to be here dedicated to the great task remaining before us–that from these honored dead we take increased devotion to that cause for which they gave the last full measure of devotion--that we here highly resolve that these dead shall not have died in vain, that this nation under God shall have a new birth of freedom, and that government of the people, by the people, for the people shall not perish from the earth.

In this passage Lincoln is saying that no one will remember his speech (of course, we know he was wrong about that). Lincoln believes that instead of his speech, people will remember those who died. He also believes that the living must work to rebuild the nation and finish the work that the soldiers died for.

The Documents

Today, there are five copies of the Gettysburg Address in Abraham Lincoln's handwriting. One copy was written before the speech and is thought to be Lincoln's first draft of the speech. This draft was given to Lincoln's private secretary, John Nicolay.

Another copy was written and revised the morning Lincoln delivered the speech. The first page of this copy was written on official White House stationery, but the second page is written in pencil on a sheet of scrap paper. It is thought that while Lincoln was satisfied with the first part of the speech on the morning of November 19, he changed the second part, which is why the second page is written on different paper. John Nicolay told someone that the second page, written in pencil, contained changes made in Gettysburg. It is this second draft that most historians believe Lincoln had with him when he made the speech in Gettysburg. This second draft was given to John Hay, Lincoln's other secretary, but Nicolay's and Hay's descendants later gave these two copies to the Library of Congress.

In 1864, a publisher asked Lincoln to write the speech again. The publisher wanted to put Lincoln's and Everett's speeches into a book that he planned to sell to raise money for wounded Civil War soldiers. This third copy of the speech is called the "third autograph copy." Today, it is in the Abraham Lincoln Presidential Library and Museum.

A fireworks display outside the Abraham Lincoln Presidential Library and Museum in Springfield, Illinois.

The Lincoln Bedroom in the White House as it looks today.

In April of 1864, George Bancroft asked Lincoln to write another copy of the speech. Bancroft planned to put this version in a book he was producing called *Autograph Leaves of Our Country's Authors*, to be sold at the Soldiers' and Sailors' Sanitary Fair in Baltimore, Maryland. Lincoln sent a page with words written on both sides of the page, which the publisher could not use, because he wanted to paste down the page onto a larger sheet of paper. He kept the copy, however. It is known as the "Bancroft copy." Years after Lincoln wrote this version, the Bancroft family donated the copy to the Cornell University Library.

Lincoln rewrote the speech on two sheets of paper for Bancroft to be put into the book. He also signed that copy—it is the only copy of the speech with Lincoln's signature. Because the book *Autograph Leaves* was bought by the Bliss family, it is called the "Bliss Copy" by historians who keep track of important documents. Today, the Bliss copy is on a desk in the Lincoln bedroom of the White House. When Lincoln was in the White House, the room was used as Lincoln's office, not as a bedroom.

The War Ends

Lincoln was elected to a second term as president in November of 1864 and was inaugurated in March 1865. The Civil War continued, but by March seemed to be winding down. Both armies had lost thousands of men and the Confederate Army, in particular, was running out of supplies and weapons.

Soldiers in front of the courthouse at Appomattox Court House, Virginia.

In February 1865, Confederate troops surrendered the port city of Charleston. Union troops had been bombing the fort for more than a year.

Union troops also concentrated on taking the Confederate capital of Richmond, Virginia. On April 2, General Lee ordered Confederate troops out of Richmond. He sent them to Amelia Court House, Virginia, where they were to get more supplies. But General Grant's troops anticipated their movements, intercepted supplies, and blocked their way.

Finally, on April 9, General Lee and the Confederate Army surrendered near Appomattox Court House, Virginia. Union troops were holding back Confederates when a Confederate soldier on horseback galloped out of the lines holding a white flag.

General Lee and General Grant arranged a meeting in the parlor of a nearby private home in the town of Appomattox Court House. The two men who had heard so much about each other but had never met except on the battlefield talked for a while, then got down to business and wrote out the terms of surrender. After the surrender Grant ordered his troops not to celebrate. The Confederate soldiers they had taken were now their prisoners, and Grant did not think it right for Americans to celebrate about taking other Americans as prisoner. Most **federal** soldiers, however, were so happy about the end of the war that they rejoiced.

On April 12, under the direction of General Grant, Confederate soldiers laid down their arms in a formal ceremony at Appomattox Court House. People all over the nation rejoiced. The war that had lasted for four years and killed more than half a million Americans was over. They realized there was now great work to do to heal the nation and bring the Confederate states back into the Union. But for awhile they celebrated. Their joy did not last long, though—only a few days after the war ended, the nation had to face another tragedy.

One family's war

The first battle of the Civil War, the Battle of Bull Run, took place in Manassas, Virginia. The battle was fought on the property of a man named Wilmer McLean. McLean moved his family to Appomattox Court House, Virginia to get away from the fighting. The war seemed to follow the McLeans. The peace agreement between the Union and the Confederacy was signed in the living room of McLean's house.

The McLean family home where the peace agreement ending the Civil War was signed.

Lincoln Assassinated

With the war over, Lincoln knew there was a lot of work to do to rebuild the broken nation. He never got to do any of the work himself. On the evening of April 14, 1865, just five days after surrender, Lincoln and his wife, Mary, went to Ford's Theater in Washington, D.C. While everyone in the audience was watching the play, an actor named John Wilkes Booth snuck into the President's box and shot Lincoln in the head. Another man tried to grab onto Booth, but Booth cut the man's arm, then jumped from the box onto the stage and shouted "*Sic Semper Tyrannus*," which is the state motto of Virginia and means "Thus always to **tyrants**." In the confusion, Booth escaped.

Lincoln was carried across the street to a private home and laid on a bed in a tiny back bedroom. As the night wore on, Lincoln grew weaker and weaker. Early in the morning, nine hours after he was shot, he died.

Booth hated the president for freeing the slaves and for suggesting in a speech on April 11 that it might be a good idea to give some blacks the right to vote. He also hated that the Confederacy lost the war and hoped that by killing Lincoln he might give the Confederates another chance. Trying to get rid of the most important people in the **federal** government, Booth also planned to kill the vice president, Andrew Johnson, and Secretary of State William Seward. Another man who was in on the plan was going to kill Johnson, but changed his mind. He did, however, find Seward, who was in bed recovering from an accident. He beat Seward, but Seward survived.

The theater box were Lincoln was assasinated.

Lincoln's funeral parade on Pennsylvania Avenue.

Several other people were convicted of working with Booth to plan the president's murder. Booth was captured on April 26, and all of those convicted of planning the murders of Lincoln, Johnson, and Seward were hanged on July 7, 1865.

Lincoln's death was a blow to the nation. He had led them through one of the most difficult periods in United States history, and in the end his goal of preserving the Union had been met. He had proved himself to be a great leader, and most Americans had hoped he would lead the country out of war and into the next phase, when the nation rebuilt and the Confederate states eased back into the Union. This period in American history is called Reconstruction.

Lincoln's vice president, Andrew Johnson, became president after Lincoln died. Johnson was not as concerned with equality as Lincoln was, and he did not support laws that helped freed slaves and other people who needed help after the war.

Know It!

The period after the Civil War is called Reconstruction and lasted until the last federal troops left the South in 1877.

The Legacy of the Gettysburg Address

When Lincoln said, "The world will little note nor long remember what we say here..." he was wrong. The Gettysburg Address is one of the most famous speeches given by a United States president. Politicians and humorists have studied and parodied the speech for generations. John F. Kennedy studied the speech before writing his inaugural address. Martin Luther King Jr.'s famous "I Have a Dream" speech references The Gettysburg Address when he says "Five score years ago..."

Many people believe that the short speech perfectly captures the feelings the country had about the Civil War. The speech defines the Civil War as being about the ideals of freedom and justice set forth in the **Declaration of Independence**. Lincoln's work to keep the Union together, and to achieve equality for all Americans, including former slaves makes him one of the most beloved former presidents in United States history.

Martin Luther King Jr.'s "I Have a Dream" speech references the Gettysburg Address.

Remembering Lincoln

There are many roads and towns named after Lincoln, especially in his home state of Illinois. Statues honor the "Great Emancipator" in all parts of the country. Construction began on the Lincoln Memorial in Washington, D.C. on February 12, 1914 (Lincoln's birthday). The statue of Lincoln inside the memorial is 19 feet (5.79 meters) tall and 19 feet wide. It is made up of 18 separate blocks of white Georgia marble. Murals depicting Lincoln's life are located on the north and south walls of the memorial. There are also inscriptions of the Gettysburg Address and Lincoln's second inaugural address. Thirty-six marble columns (one for each state at the time of Lincoln's death) surround the memorial. The memorial was **dedicated** in 1922. The event was attended by many Civil War veterans and Robert Todd Lincoln, Lincoln's only surviving son.

Know It!

The Library of Congress had two special containers built to store their two copies of the Gettysburg Address. The containers are filled with gas to keep oxygen out of the container. This keeps the documents from deteriorating. The containers are kept at 49.5° F (9.7° C).

The Lincoln Memorial in Washington D.C. is a popular tourist site.

Gettysburg National Military Park

The cemetery **dedicated** by Lincoln on November 19, 1863, became Gettysburg National Military Park in 1895. Today, the park covers nearly 3,000 acres. More than 1,400 monuments, markers, and memorials can be found there. The park is open every day of the year, and in the visitors center is a museum where guests can see models of the great battle. Hundreds of cannons from the Civil War are in the park, positioned near where they were during the actual battle. Visitors can see the site where Lincoln delivered the Gettysburg Address and the headquarters of Robert E. Lee.

For years after the Civil War, veterans would gather in Gettysburg to remember the great battle that was fought there. As late as 1913, 54,000 former soldiers—both Union and Confederate—gathered at Gettysburg on the 50th anniversary of the battle. Each year, almost two million people visit the park. The National Park Service is in charge of taking care of the park today.

Gettysburg military camps in 1913

Gettysburg National Battlefield Park as it looks today.

MP JULY 1-2-3-1913 PHOTO G.S.CARNEY COPYRIGHTED
268 W-WATER ST MILWAUKEE WISCONSIN

Glossary

abolitionists people who worked to end slavery

artifact object made and used by someone in the past

bombard to attack with weapons for a long period of time

Congress lawmaking body of the United States government

conservator person who is responsible for the care, restoration, and repair of documents and other historical artifacts

Declaration of Independence document in which the American colonies formally declared independence from Great Britain in 1776

debate formal discussion in which two sides of an issue are represented; (v) to take part in a debate

dedicate set something aside for a special use

deteriorate become damaged in quality, condition, or value

draft unfinished form of a piece of writing

economy system of buying and selling; how a country makes money

export product bought by one country from another

federal one central government that oversees smaller units; the smaller units, such as states, have their own governments. Union soldiers were sometimes called federal troops, or just federals.

inauguration ceremony during which the United States president is officially sworn in

legislature group of elected individuals who make laws for those who elect them

merchant shop owner or trader

military group formed to fight or protect, such as army or air force

plantation large farm, usually in the South

podium upright stand speakers stand behind when teaching or giving a speech

secede leave or separate

secretary of state person in the United States government who is responsible for foreign affairs

siege surround an opposing army and capture it by bombing and blockading it

strategy plan or tactic used to achieve a goal

territory part of the United States that is not a state. Many present states were first territories.

tyrant leader who ignores the law and follows his own rules

unconstitutional going against the United States Constitution, which is the document of written law upon which the United States government is based

More Books to Read

Burke, Rick. *Abraham Lincoln.* Chicago: Heinemann Library, 2002.

Feinberg, Barbara Silberdick. *Abraham Lincoln's Gettysburg Address: Four Score and More.* Brookfield, Conn.: Milbrook, 2000

Rivera, Sheila. *The Gettysburg Address.* Edina, Minn.: ABDO, 2004.

Places to Visit

Gettysburg National Military Park
Gettysburg, PA 17325
(717) 334-1124
www.nps.gov/gett/

Index